Super Safari 3

Letters and Numbers Workbook

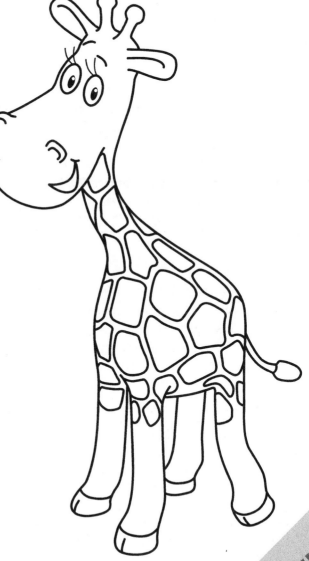

CAMBRIDGE
UNIVERSITY PRESS

T0159711

Colour in Gina!

Shaftesbury Road, Cambridge CB2 8EA, United Kingdom

One Liberty Plaza, 20th Floor, New York, NY 10006, USA

477 Williamstown Road, Port Melbourne, VIC 3207, Australia

314–321, 3rd Floor, Plot 3, Splendor Forum, Jasola District Centre, New Delhi – 110025, India

103 Penang Road, #05–06/07, Visioncrest Commercial, Singapore 238467

Cambridge University Press & Assessment is a department of the University of Cambridge.

We share the University's mission to contribute to society through the pursuit of education, learning and research at the highest international levels of excellence.

www.cambridge.org
Information on this title: www.cambridge.org/9781316628188

First published 2016

20 19 18 17 16 15 14 13 12 11 10

Printed in Great Britain by CPI Group (UK) Ltd, Croydon CR0 4YY

A catalogue record for this publication is available from the British Library

ISBN   978-1-316-62818-8 Paperback

Additional resources for this publication at www.cambridge.org/supersafari

Super Safari 3

Letters and Numbers Workbook

Hello!

The children draw their face. Write each child's name with a grey pencil. The children trace their name with coloured pencils.

1 **Draw and trace.**

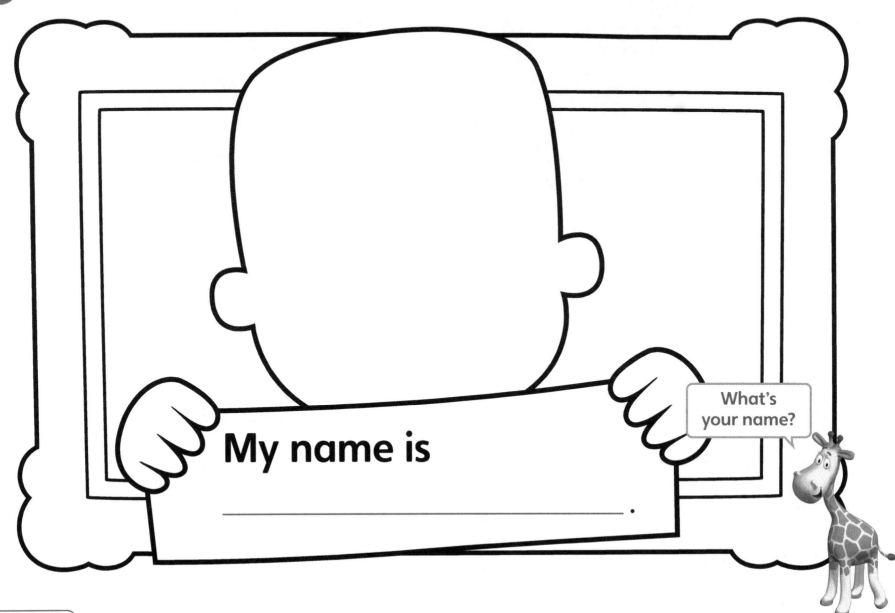

My name is

What's your name?

1 **Connect the dots. Colour the bag.**

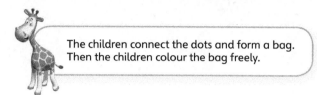

The children connect the dots and form a bag. Then the children colour the bag freely.

1 My classroom

1 Trace the letters.

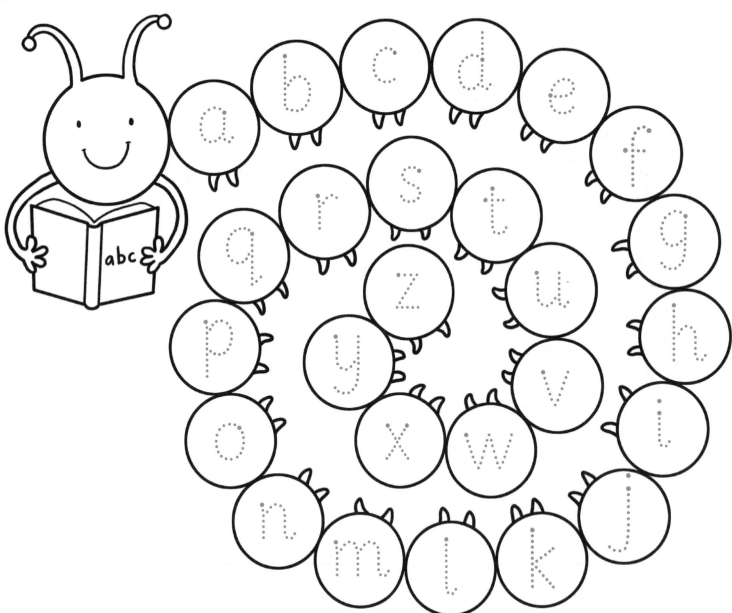

1 **Count, circle and colour.**

Review the numbers from 1 to 5. Next, the children count the objects in each box and circle the corresponding number. Finally, the children colour the objects and numbers freely.

2 / 5   4 / 3   2 / 1

1 / 4   4 / 5   5 / 3

1 **Look and match. Colour the pictures.**

Review the alphabet. Then the children look at the letters and match them with the corresponding pictures. Finally, the children colour the pictures freely.

a c e g j m

1 **Colour the correct number of objects.**

Review the numbers from 1 to 10. Then the children point to the number 9 and colour nine crayons. Repeat the procedure for the remaining numbers and items.

9

8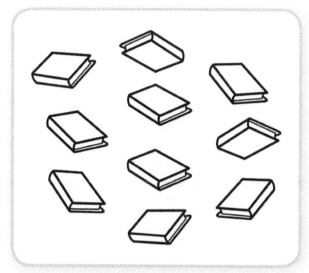

6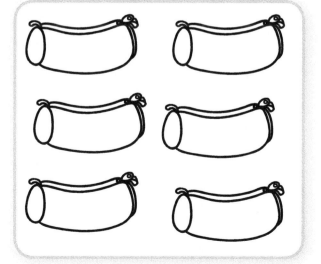

7

1 **Look, mark and colour.**

n   j   f   l

☐   ☐   ☐   ☐

d   t   r   q

☐   ☐   ☐   ☐

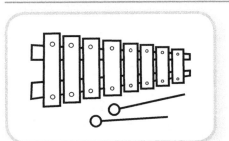

w   x   v   y

☐   ☐   ☐   ☐

b   s   z   k

☐   ☐   ☐   ☐

1 **Write the missing numbers. Colour.**

Review the numbers from 1 to 10. Then the children look at the first series of numbers and write the missing number. Repeat the procedure for the remaining series. Finally, the children colour the pictures freely.

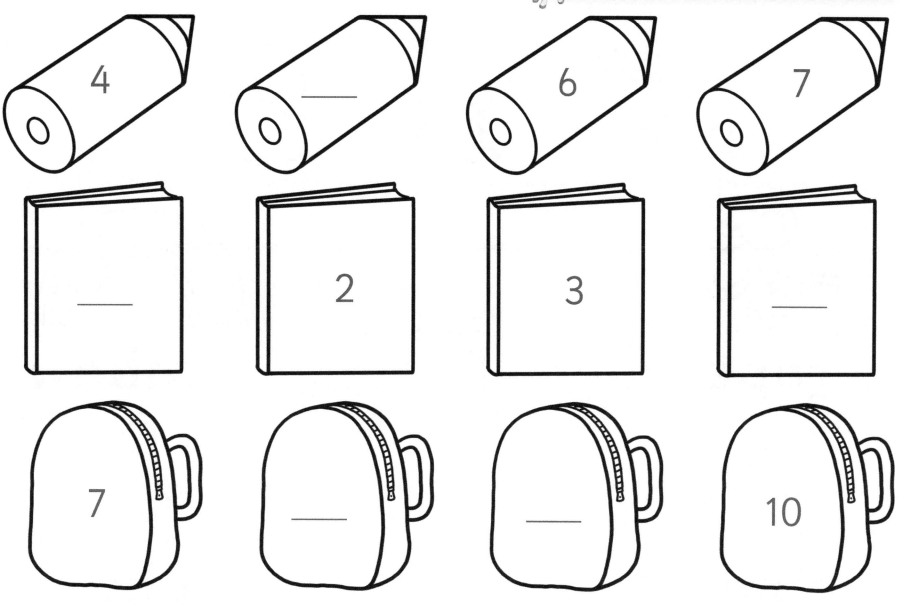

4   ___   6   7

___   2   3   ___

7   ___   ___   10

My numbers   11

1 **Listen and match. Colour the pictures.**

Say /r/ – /r/ – /r/ – *rabbit*. Repeat with *red*. Next, ask *Does rope begin with the /r/ sound? Yes!* The children match *rope* with the letter "r". Continue in the same manner with the rest of the activity. Finally, the children colour the pictures freely.

r

rope

rainbow

r

ring

robot

1 Colour, glue and cut. Play.

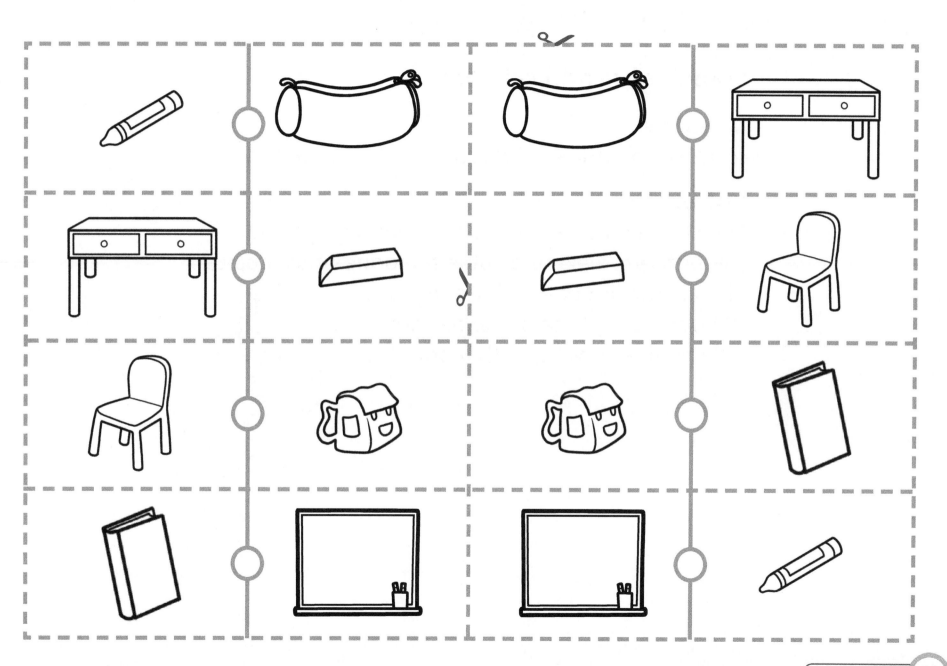

Colour, glue and cut. Play.

Materials:

construction paper, glue, scissors, coloured pencils

Instructions:

The children identify the classroom objects and colour them. Next, they glue the page onto a piece of construction paper. Once dry, the children cut out the dominoes and play on their own or with a partner.

1 **Listen. Colour the pictures.**

Say *The chair is blue*. The children colour the chair blue. Repeat the procedure for the following items: pencil–yellow, rubber–red, book–green, bag–orange, desk–purple.

2 My family

The children identify the family members. Then the children trace the words with coloured pencils. Finally, the children colour the pictures freely.

1 Trace. Colour the pictures.

grandpa

grandma

dad

mum

sister

brother

1 Connect the dots. Colour the house.

Review the numbers from 1 to 20. Say *Families live in houses*. Next, the children connect the dots. Ask *What is it? A house!* Finally, the children colour the house freely.

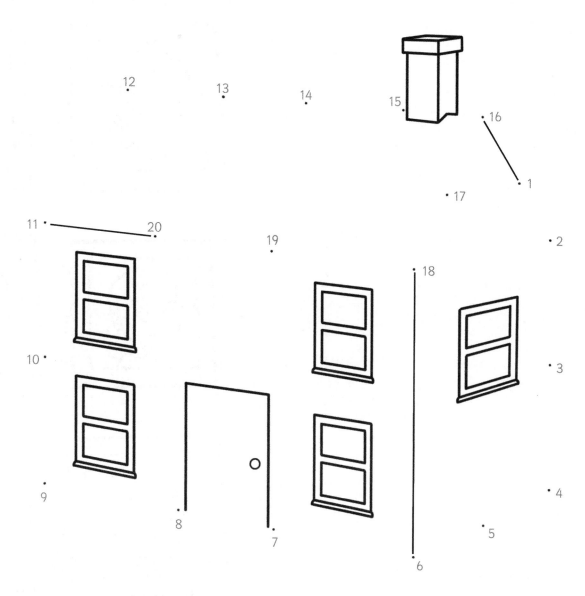

1 **Trace. Colour the correct frame.**

The children trace the words with coloured pencils. Then they colour the corresponding frames.

This is my grandpa.

This is my grandma.

This is my dad.

1 **Count and match. Colour the pictures.**

10 4 14 20

The children trace the words with coloured pencils. Then the children match the sentences with the corresponding pictures. Finally, the children colour the pictures freely.

This is my mum.

This is my sister.

This is my brother.

1 Count. Write the numbers.

Review the numbers from 10 to 20. Then the children count the objects in each box and write the corresponding number on the lines.

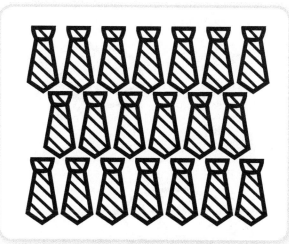

_____

_____

_____

_____

_____

_____

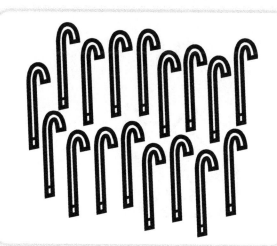

1 **Listen and trace. Colour the pictures.**

Say /f/ – /f/ – /f/ – *fish*, *family*. Then the children trace the letter "f" in each word. Next, they say each word aloud. Finally, the children colour the pictures freely.

f an

f lower

f oot

f ox

f ork

f rog

1 Make and assemble a puzzle.

Make and assemble a puzzle.

Materials:
construction paper, glue, coloured pencils, scissors

Instructions:
The children colour the scene. Then they glue the page onto a piece of construction paper. Next, they cut out the scene along the dotted lines to make puzzle pieces. Finally, the children assemble the puzzle.

1 **Read and circle. Colour the pictures.**

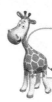

The children look at the pictures and circle the correct words. Then they colour the pictures freely.

dad / mum

sister / brother

grandma / grandpa

dad / mum

grandpa / brother

sister / grandpa

3 My face

The children trace over each path with a red crayon. Next, they trace the corresponding words with coloured pencils. Finally, the children colour the pictures.

1 Follow, match and trace. Colour.

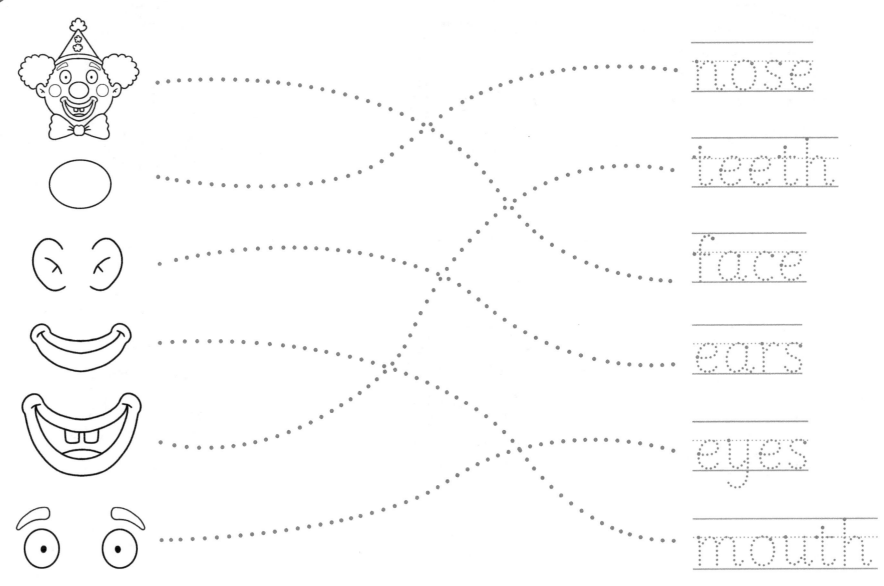

nose

teeth

face

ears

eyes

mouth

1 **Count and colour the numbers.**

Present the numbers. The children count the mouths and ears in each box. Next, the children colour the numbers freely.

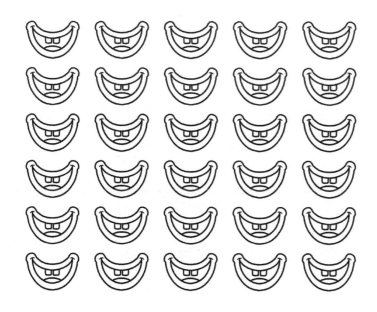

30

40

1 **Trace and match. Colour the pictures.**

The children trace the words with coloured pencils.
Next, the children match the sentences with the corresponding pictures.
Finally, the children colour the pictures freely.

This is my mouth.

This is my nose.

This is my face.

1 **Count and circle the correct number.**

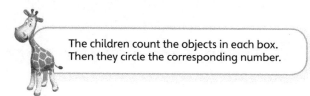

The children count the objects in each box.
Then they circle the corresponding number.

30/40   30/40

1 **Trace. Circle the correct picture.**

The children trace the words with coloured pencils. Next, the children circle the correct pictures. Finally, the children colour the pictures they circled.

They're my eyes.

They're my ears.

They're my teeth.

1 **Draw five more.**

= **30**

= **40**

1 **Listen and write. Colour the pictures.**

Say /h/ – /h/ – /h/ – hat, happy. Does hen begin with the /h/ sound? Yes! Next, the children write a letter "h" at the beginning of hen. Repeat for house and hand. Finally, the children colour the pictures freely.

___en

___ouse

___and

1 Colour the faces. Cut out and assemble.

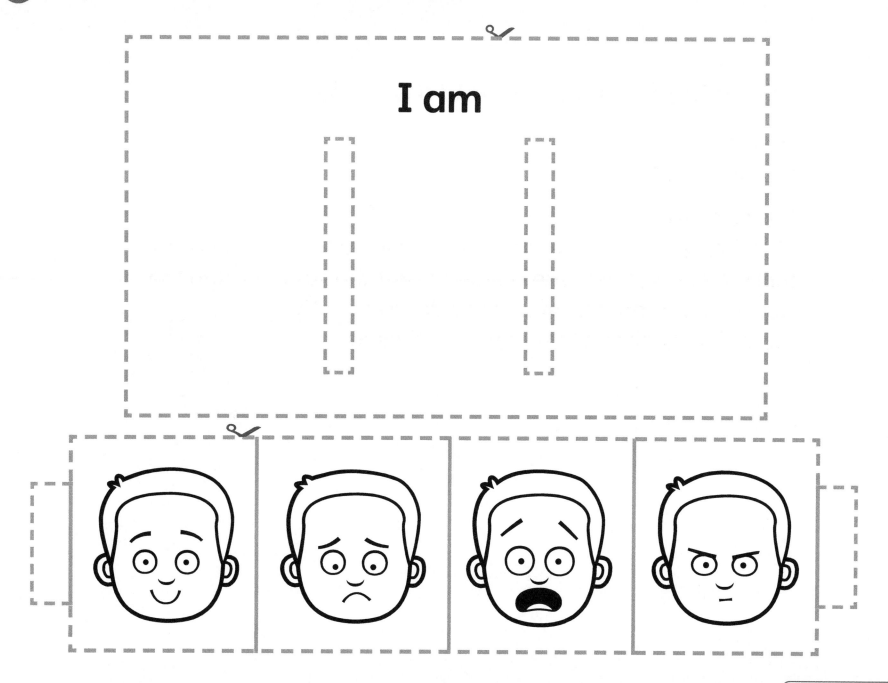

I am

Colour the faces. Cut out and assemble.

Materials:
scissors, crayons

Instructions:
The children colour the faces. Next, they cut out the slits and make two slots. Help the children insert the strip through the slots and pull on it from side to side to move the faces. Finally, the children say how they feel.

1 **Read and match. Colour the picture.**

 The children match the words with the corresponding parts of the picture. Then the children colour the clown's face freely.

eyes

face

ears

teeth

nose

mouth

4 My toys

The children write the words in the boxes.
Then the children colour the toys freely.

1 Write. Colour the toys.

plane rope kite doll ball

1 **Count and match. Colour the numbers.**

The children count the toys in each box and match the boxes with the corresponding numbers. Then the children colour the numbers freely.

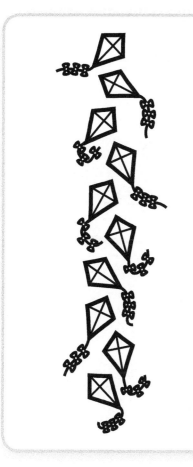

30 40 10 20

1 **Circle and write. Colour the pictures.**

The children circle the corresponding word under each picture. Then they copy the words onto the lines. Finally, the children colour the pictures freely.

doll   teddy bear

I have a _____ .

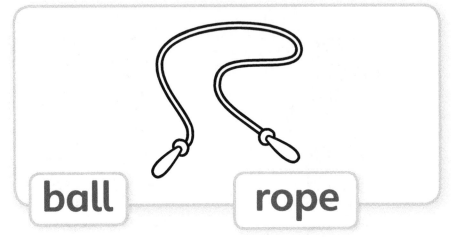

ball   rope

I have a _____ .

plane   kite

I have a _____ .

1 **Count and circle.**

The children count the toys in each box. Then they circle the corresponding number.

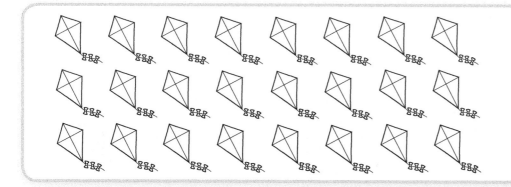

20/24

33/35

29/40

1 **Mark the correct word. Write.**

The children look at the first picture and mark the word that best completes the first sentence. Then they copy the word onto the line. Repeat the procedure for the remaining pictures and sentences. Finally, the children colour the pictures freely.

We have a _____ .

☐ rope   ☐ kite

We have a _____ .

☐ ball   ☐ plane

We have a _____ .

☐ teddy bear   ☐ doll

1 Write the missing numbers. Colour.

The children complete the two series of numbers. Then they colour the pictures freely.

1 **Listen. Colour the correct pictures.**

Say /g/ – /g/ – /g/ – dog, dig. Colour the pictures that end with the /g/ sound. Does bag end with the /g/ sound? Yes! Then the children colour the picture of the bag. Continue in the same manner with the rest of the activity.

g

ba<u>g</u>

ba<u>t</u>

fla<u>g</u>

fi<u>sh</u>

bu<u>g</u>

wi<u>n</u>

1 Colour, cut out and glue. Assemble.

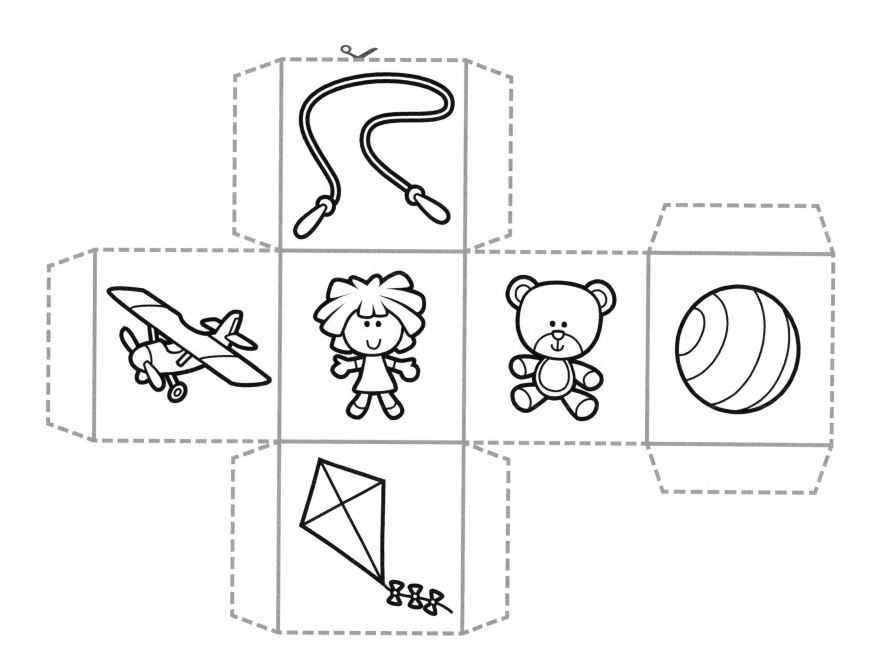

Colour, cut out and glue. Assemble.

Materials:
scissors, coloured pencils, glue

Instructions:
The children colour the pictures. Then they cut out the cube and assemble it. Then pair the children. The children take turns rolling the cubes and identifying the toys.

1 Read. Colour the correct picture.

Read the word *plane*. The children read along. Then the children look at the pictures and colour the one that depicts a toy plane. Repeat the procedure for the remaining words and pictures.

plane

teddy bear

doll

rope

5 My house

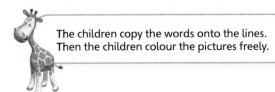

The children copy the words onto the lines.
Then the children colour the pictures freely.

1 **Write. Colour the pictures.**

bath

cupboard

bed

1 **Count and colour.**

 Present the number 50. The children count the petals in each flower. Finally, the children colour the flowers freely.

10   20   30   40

50

1 **Trace, write and colour.**

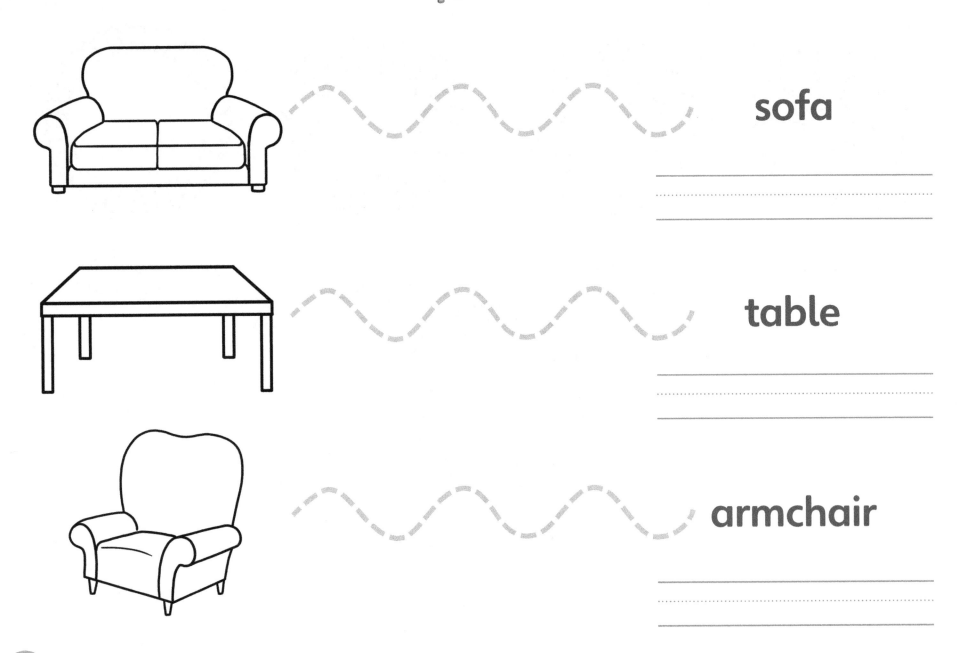

sofa

table

armchair

1 Count and colour.

Present the number. Next, the children count the bubbles in the baths in sets of tens. Finally, the children colour the pictures freely.

60

1 **Write. Colour the pictures.**

The children copy the words *cupboard*, *bed* and *table* onto the lines to complete each sentence. Then they colour the pictures freely.

cupboard

The ball is in the _____.

bed

The kite is on the _____.

table

The doll is under the _____.

The children count the kites and circle the correct number. Repeat the procedure for the armchairs.

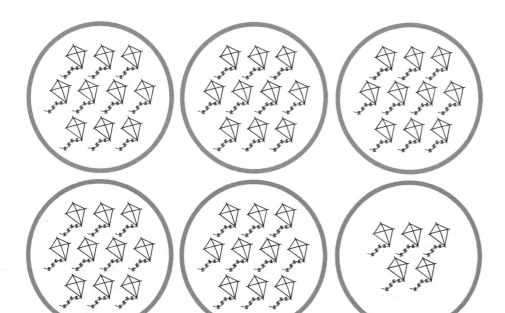

= **55   53   60**

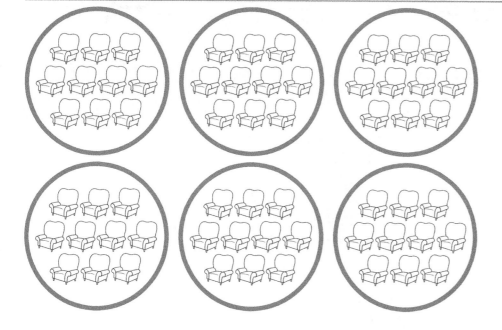

= **58   60   57**

1 **Listen, write and colour.**

Say /j/ – /j/ – /j/ – yogurt – yellow. Does yarn begin with the /j/ sound? Yes! Write the letter "y" on the lines to complete the word yarn. Then say Does jacket begin with the /j/ sound? No! Do not write the letter "y". Continue in the same manner with the rest of the activity. Next, the children read aloud the words that begin with the /j/ sound: yarn, yawn, yak. Finally, the children colour only the pictures that begin with the /j/ sound.

arn

acket

awn

ar

ak

1 Cut out and play.

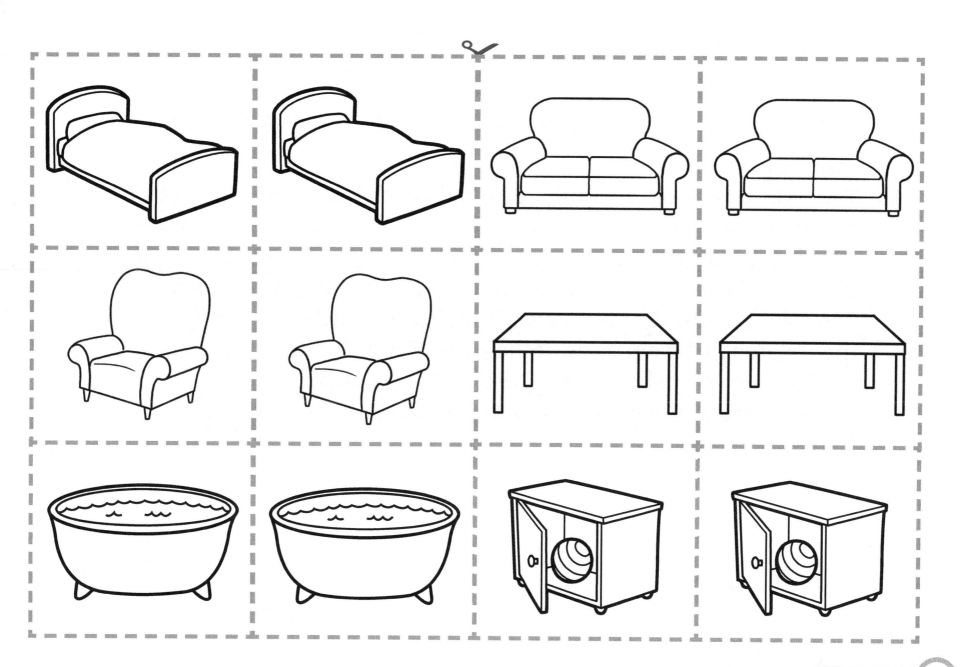

Cut out and play.

Materials:

scissors, coloured pencils, glue, piece of construction paper (1 per child)

Instructions:

The children colour the furniture items in each box. Then they detach the page and glue it onto a piece of construction paper. Once dry, the children cut out the boxes to make memory cards. The children shuffle the cards. Then they put the cards face down in rows on a table. The children turn over two cards. If the cards match, the children put them aside. If they do not match, the children turn them back over. The children continue playing until all the matching cards are found.

1 **Complete, circle and colour.**

The children look at the pictures and complete them. Then they circle the correct word. Finally, the children colour the pictures freely.

sofa / table

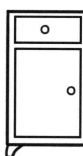

bed / cupboard

armchair / bed

sofa / bath

table / bed

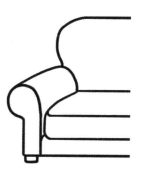

cupboard / sofa

6 On the farm

The children trace the sentences. Next, the children draw and colour the animals' missing parts. Finally, the children colour the animals freely.

1 Trace. Draw the missing parts. Colour.

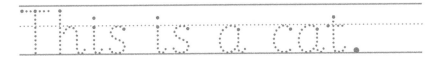

1 **Count. Paint the number.**

Present the number. Next, the children count the sheep by tens. Finally, the children paint the number 70 with watercolours.

1 **Trace, match and colour.**

The children trace the sentences with coloured pencils. Next, the children match the sentences to the corresponding pictures. Finally, the children colour the pictures freely.

This is a cow.

This is a rabbit.

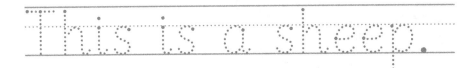
This is a sheep.

1 **Count and colour.**

 Present the number. Next, the children count the dots on the butterflies in sets of ten. Finally, the children colour the dots on each butterfly freely.

80

1 **Trace and draw.**

The children trace the sentences. Then the children illustrate each sentence.

I like cats.

I like dogs.

I like horses.

1 **Connect the dots. Colour the rabbit.**

Review the numbers from 1 to 80. Then the children connect the dots and form a rabbit. Finally, the children colour the rabbit freely.

1 **Listen, match and colour.**

Say /z/ – /z/ – /z/ – zebra – zoo. Ask *Does zip start with the /z/ sound? Yes! Match zip with the letter "z".* Continue in the same manner with the rest of the activity. Finally, the children colour the pictures freely.

zip

zero

z

zigzag

zeppelin

1 Make finger puppets.

Make finger puppets.

Materials:
coloured crayons, scissors, tape

Instructions:
The children colour each animal. Next, the children cut out the animals. Help the children join the ends of the tabs with tape. Make sure the puppets adjust to the children's fingers. Finally, the children play with their finger puppets.

1 **Colour the farm animals. Match.**

The children colour the farm animals. Next, the children match the pictures to the corresponding words.

cat

horse

cow

dog

rabbit

sheep

7 I'm hungry!

The children trace the sentences and mark the correct pictures. Next, the children colour the pictures they marked.

1 Trace, mark and colour.

 ☐ ☐

 ☐ ☐

 ☐  ☐

1 Count and write the number.

The children identify and count the cakes. Then they write the total number of cakes on the line. Repeat the same procedure for the remaining food items. Finally, the children colour the pictures freely.

 _____

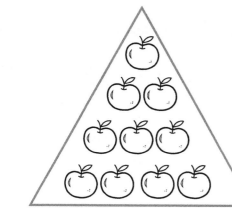 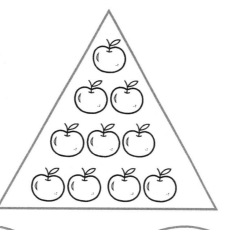

 _____

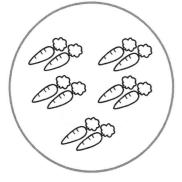 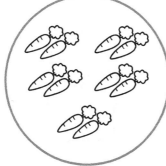 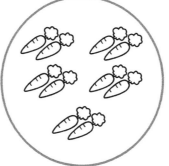

 _____

1 **Trace. Cross out the correct picture.**

The children trace the sentences. Next, the children cross out the corresponding picture. Finally, the children colour the pictures they crossed out.

I don't like sausages.

I don't like ice cream.

I don't like chips.

1 **Count, write and colour.**

The children count the food items in each box. Then they write the corresponding amount of food items next to each picture. Finally, the children colour the apple, the sausage and the carrot freely.

How many?

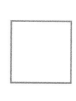

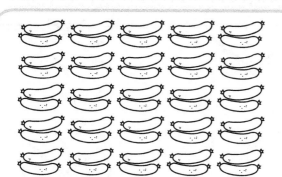

1 **Trace. Circle and colour the correct picture.**

The children trace the sentences. Then the children circle and colour the correct pictures.

I like apples.

I don't like cake.

I don't like ice cream.

I don't like sausages.

1 **Write the missing numbers. Colour.**

Review the numbers from 10 to 80. Next, the children look at the picture and write the missing numbers. Finally, the children colour the picture freely.

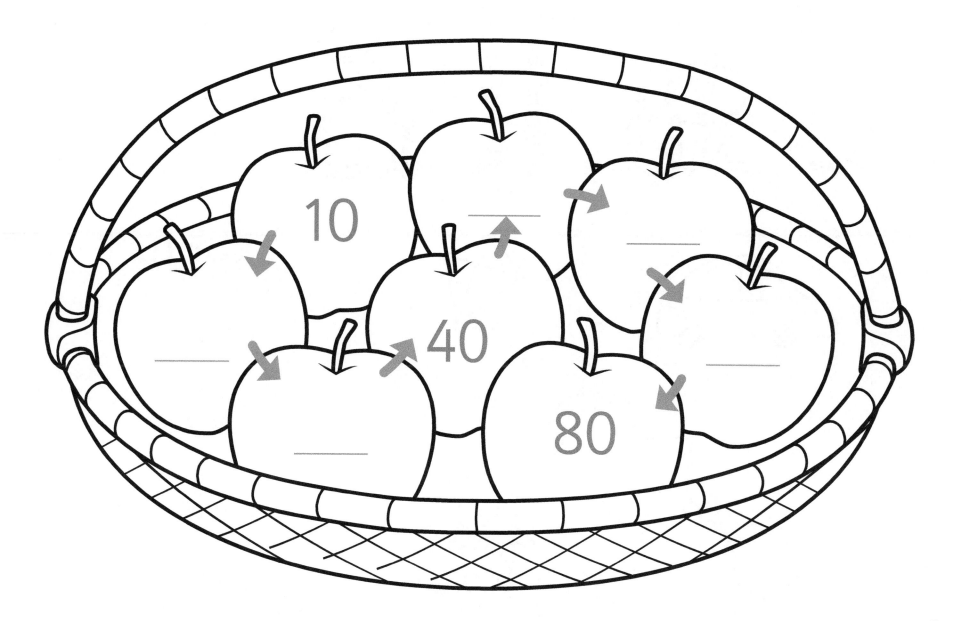

1 **Listen, match and colour.**

 Say /k/ – /k/ – /k/ – cat – king. Next, say the words car, kite, cap, key and koala. Next, the children match the pictures to the corresponding words. Then the children find the letter "c" or "k" in each word. Finally, the children colour the pictures freely.

<u>k</u>oala

<u>c</u>ar

<u>k</u>ey

<u>c</u>ap

<u>k</u>ite

1 Colour and cut out. Sort.

I like

I don't like

Colour and cut out. Sort.

Materials:
coloured pencils, scissors, glue

Instructions:
The children identify the food items and colour them. Next, they cut them out. The children glue the food items onto the corresponding column, depending on whether they like them or not.

1 Circle the correct word. Colour.

The children look at the patterns and identify the food items. Then the children circle the word that comes next in each pattern. Finally, they colour the pictures freely.

     **carrots / apples**

 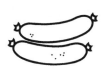   **sausages / chips**

     **carrots / cake**

      **apples / sausages**

       ice cream / chips

The children copy the sentences onto the lines. Next, the children colour the pictures freely.

1 **Read and write. Colour the pictures.**

I'm riding a bike.

I'm riding a scooter.

I'm driving a car.

1 **Count and colour.**

1 **Circle, write and colour.**

The children circle the correct pictures. Then the children copy the sentences onto the lines. Finally, the children colour the pictures freely.

You're flying a plane.

You're sailing a boat.

1 ## Count. Colour the number.

Present the number. The children count the windows on the buses in sets of ten. Then they colour the number 100 freely.

 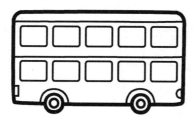  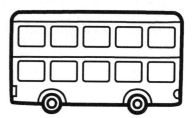

 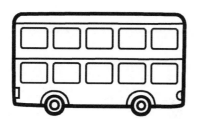  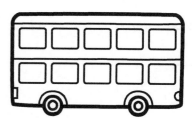

100

1 **Mark, write and colour.**

The children look at the pictures. Then they mark the correct speech bubbles. Next, they copy the corresponding sentences onto the lines. Finally, they colour the pictures freely.

I'm driving a train.

I'm driving a bus.

I'm riding a bike.

I'm sailing a boat.

1 Count. Circle the correct number.

Review the numbers from 10 to 100. Then the children count the stars on the boats and circle the corresponding number. Repeat the procedure for the windows on the buses.

How many?

90   95   93

100   90   95

1 **Listen and trace. Colour the pictures.**

Say /ŋ/ – /ŋ/ – /ŋ/ – dancing – singing, running, riding and sailing. Next, the children connect the letters and trace the arrows from the letters to the words and from the words to the pictures. Then the children identify the letters "n" and "g" at the end of each word and trace them. Finally, the children colour the pictures freely.

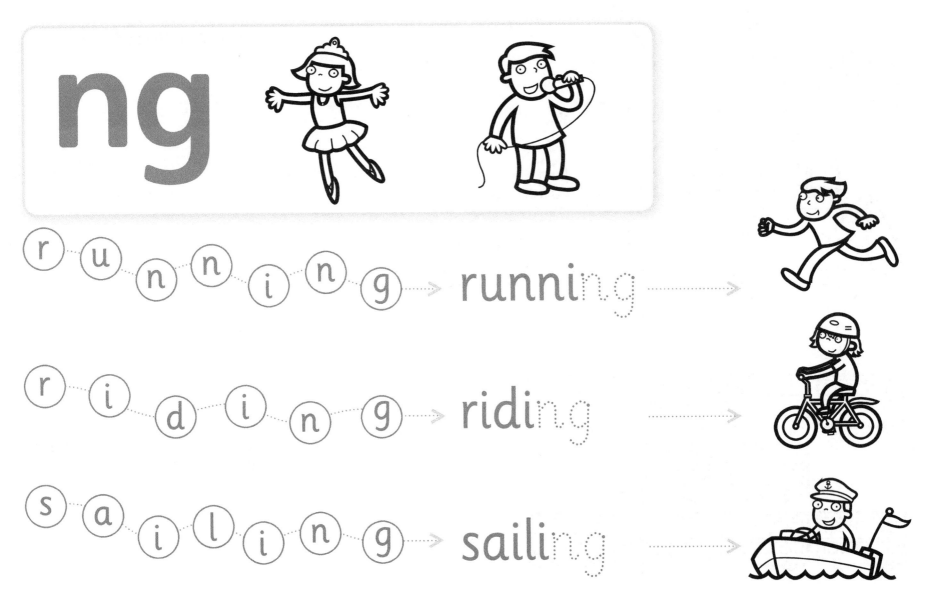

running

riding

sailing

1 Paint and cut out. Glue and assemble.

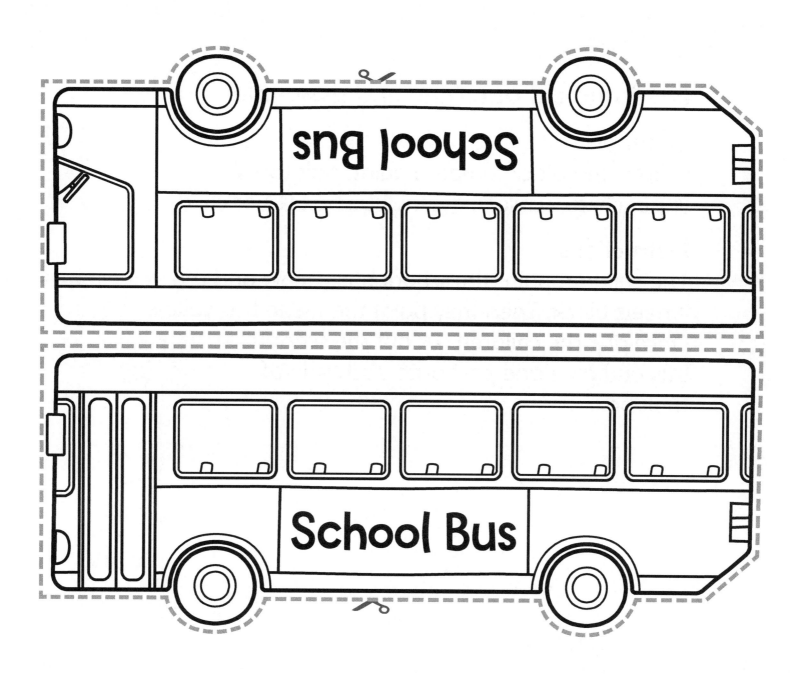

Paint and cut out. Glue and assemble.

Materials:
yellow and black tempera paint, paintbrush
(1 per child), scissors, glue, tissue box (1 per child)

Instructions:
The children paint the school bus yellow and the
wheels black. Then they paint the tissue box yellow.
Once dry, the children cut out the school
bus and glue one part onto each side of
their box.

1 Solve the puzzle.

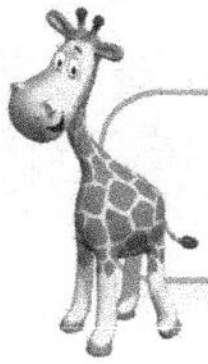

The children look at the pictures and identify the means of transportation. Then the children solve the puzzle.

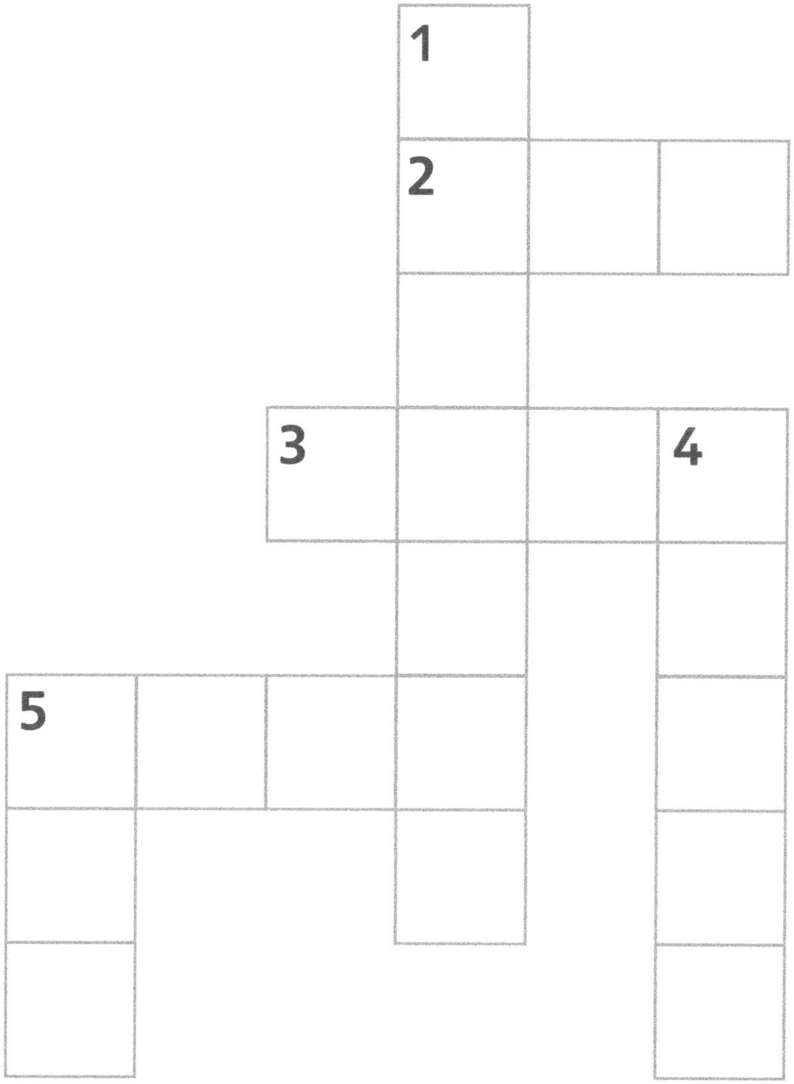

Across →

2.
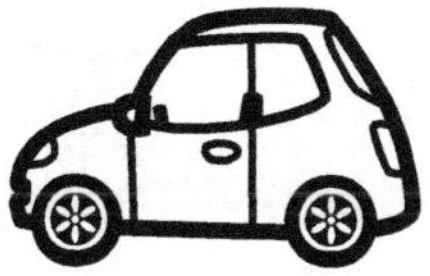

3.
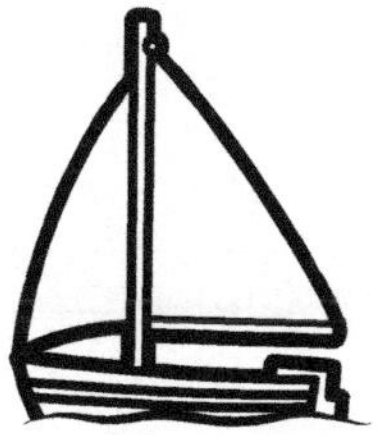

5.
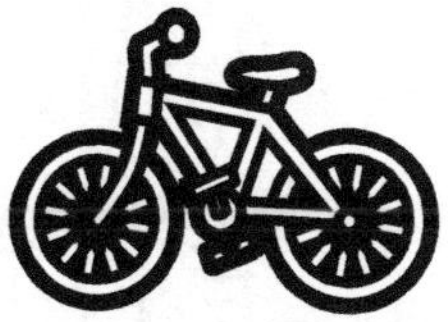

Down ↓

1.
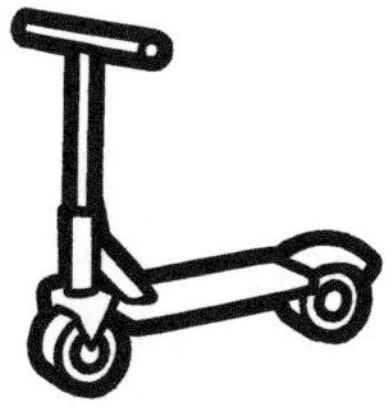

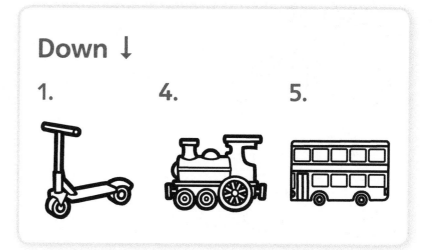

4.

5.
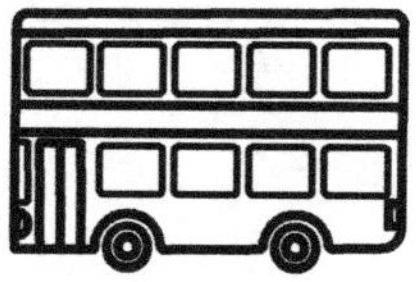

9 Party clothes

The children copy the words *I like your* onto the first line and complete the sentence with the word *boots*. Repeat the procedure for the remaining items. Finally, the children colour the pictures freely.

1 Read, write and colour.

I like your hat.

boots

shoes

buttons

1 **Write the missing numbers. Colour.**

Review the numbers from 10 to 100. Next, the children write the missing numbers on the path with coloured pencils. Finally, the children colour the picture freely.

1 Look, write and colour.

The children copy the words *He has a* and complete the sentence with the words *red* and *hat*. Repeat the procedure for the remaining sentences. Finally, the children colour the pictures freely.

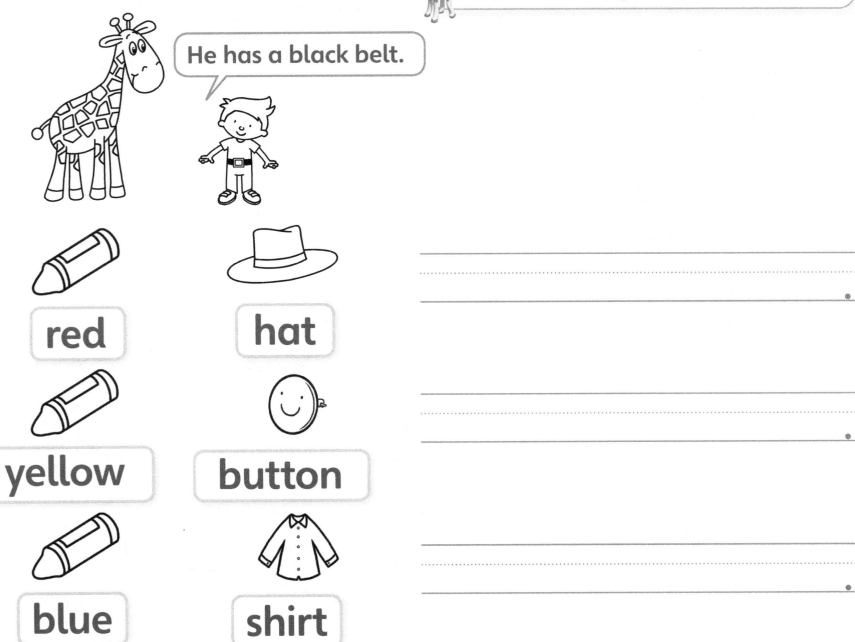

He has a black belt.

red   hat

yellow   button

blue   shirt

1 **Trace. Colour the numbers.**

10

70

20

80

60

30

90

50

40

100

1 **Trace and write. Colour the pictures.**

The children trace the arrows and connect the words to form sentences. Then they copy the sentences onto the lines. Finally, the children colour the pictures freely.

Let's ⟶ have ⟶ ice cream

Let's ⟶ have ⟶ sausages

Let's ⟶ have ⟶ chips

1 Count. Cross out the extra objects.

Say *There are twenty-two hats. We only need twenty hats. Cross out the extra hats.* The children cross out two hats. Repeat the procedure for the remaining objects.

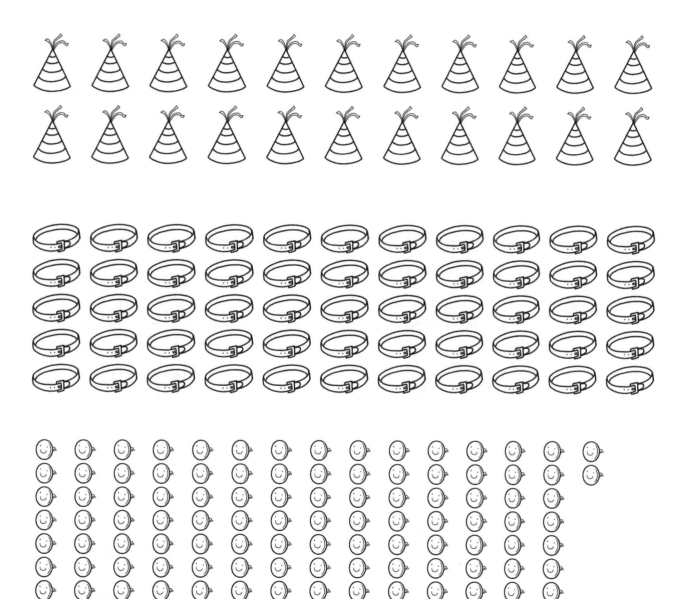

20

53

97

1 Circle the correct letter. Colour.

 Review the alphabet. Then the children look at the pictures and identify the objects. Next, the children circle the letter each word begins with. Finally, the children colour the pictures freely.

a   i

c   k

j   h

u   w

k   q

m   n

s   c

x   y

z   x

1 Colour and cut out. Dress the doll.

Colour and cut out. Dress the doll.

Materials:
piece of construction paper (1 per child), scissors, glue, coloured pencils

Instructions:
The children colour the doll and the clothing items. Then they glue the page onto a piece of construction paper. Once dry, the children cut out the doll and the clothing items. Finally, the children glue the clothes onto the doll.

1 **Match. Colour the pictures.**

The children match the letters to the corresponding lines in order to complete the words. Next, the children colour the items freely.

s__i_____

(r) (h) (t)

b__t__o__

(t) (u) (n)

__o__t__

(o) (b) (s)

__h_____s

(o) (s) (e)

Thanks and acknowledgements

The publishers are grateful to the following contributors:

Blooberry Design: cover design, book design, publishing management
and page make-up
Bill Bolton: cover illustration

The publishers and authors are grateful to the following illustrators:

Bill Bolton 1, 4, 86, 87, (1 and repeats on all pages of Gina);
Louise Gardner 5, 6, 7, 8, 9, 11, 13, 17, 21, 26, 27, 28, 29, 31, 35, 48, 52, 55,
61, 63, 65, 70, 86, 87, 88, 91, 92, 95; Marek Jagucki 4, 15, 16, 18, 19, 20,
23, 25, 33, 37, 38, 43, 45, 47, 50, 57, 58, 59, 67, 68, 69, 71, 73, 75, 78, 79, 80,
81, 83, 85, 93; Bernice Lum 8, 10, 12, 21, 22, 32, 36, 38, 39, 40, 41, 42, 45,
46, 49, 51, 52, 53, 56, 58, 62, 66, 67, 68, 69, 72, 73, 75, 76, 77, 82, 88, 90, 92